Medieval Irish Pilgrim Paths

St Kevin's Way,
Hollywood to Glendalough
Co. Wicklow

Peter Harbison and Joss Lynam

Symbol taken from stone at Ballyvourney, Co Cork.

An Chomhairle Oidhreachta / The Heritage Council

2002

© An Chomhairle Oidhreachta / The Heritage Council 2002

All rights reserved.
No part of this book may be printed or reproduced
or utilised in any electronic, mechanical, or other means,
now known or hereotafter invented,
including photocopying or licence permitting
restricted copying in Ireland issued by the
Irish Copyright Licencing Agency Ltd.,
The Writers Centre, 19 Parnell Square, Dublin 1.

Published by the Heritage Council

The assistance of the National Millennium Committee
is gratefully acknowledged.

Text by Peter Harbison and Joss Lynam.

Photographs by courtesy of
The National Museum of Ireland (p 3 and 36)
Ted Creedon (p 4, 7 and 11)
Ulster Museum, Belfast (p 34 and 35)
William Mullen (p 21)
Peter Harbison (p 22, 28, 30 and 32)
Philip Tottenham (p 38)

Cartoon by George Campbell (p 33).

Maps by Barry Dalby, East-West Mapping.

Designed and Produced by B. Magee Design.

ISSN 1393 – 68 08

The Heritage Council of Ireland Series.

ISBN 1 901137 38 4

PRICE: €6.50

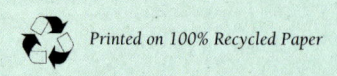

Printed on 100% Recycled Paper

CONTENTS

GENERAL WALKING INFORMATION	4
LANDKARTENFÜHRER FÜR PILGERWANDERWEGE:EINFÜHRUNG	7
CHEMINS DE PÈLERINAGE: INTRODUCTION GÉNERALE	11
USEFUL PHONE NUMBERS AND ADDRESSES	15
THE PILGRIM PATHS PROJECT	16
HISTORICAL BACKGROUND	17
KEY TO MAP SYMBOLS	19
MAIN ROUTE - START FROM HOLLYWOOD	20
ALTERNATIVE ROUTE FROM VALLEYMOUNT	26
THE OLD MONASTERY AT GLENDALOUGH	32
THE HOLLYWOOD LABYRINTH STONE	36
THE PILGRIMS' ROAD - THE TÓCHAR	37
BULLAUN STONES	38
TURLOUGH HILL ELECTRICITY GENERATING STATION	38
THE LEAD MINES	39
ACKNOWLEDGEMENTS	39
BIBLIOGRAPHY	40

General Walking Information

1. Using the Map Guide

The text and maps in this guide are designed for a walker and pilgrim starting from Hollywood and finishing in Glendalough.

The scale of the map is 1:50,000 (that is 5mm to 1 kilometre). All maps are oriented to the north.

Beside each map is a brief description of the section of the path shown on the map. For walking we suggest you fold back the guide at the relevant page and put it into the plastic wallet which will protect it from the weather.

Of necessity, the maps in the guide can only show a limited section of the countryside along the line of the Paths. We recommend that you take with you the Ordnance Survey 1:50,000 Discovery Series maps which will give you a more complete picture of the countryside. The relevant sheet is no.56.

2. Following the Paths

The path is waymarked by black recycled plastic markers, recognisable by the yellow Pilgrim Symbol, with arrows showing the direction to be taken. These arrows suit the pilgrim whichever direction he/she is walking.

Where the Path joins or leaves a public road there is a brown fingerpost with the name of the Path, and the Pilgrim Symbol.

At the start and finish, and in villages along the route, there are map boards showing the whole path.

3. Safety

This Path follows quiet roads or country tracks or paths, and poses very few dangers. However pilgrims should remember that Irish weather is changeable and that even a minor injury to leg or foot maybe difficult to deal with a few kilometres away from a public road. So make sure that you wear or carry warm clothes and wind-proof/rain-proof gear. Walking boots are not needed, but stout shoes are necessary for comfort on muddy or rough paths. In the very unlikely event of an accident requiring outside help, the emergency telephone number is 999. Please note that while walking the Path you are responsible for your own safety.

4. Access

This Path is not a Right of Way apart from the stretches on public roads. Off the road it crosses private property by courtesy of the owner who may withdraw permission if users of the Path create difficulties for his/her farming or other work.

So please respect the owner's generosity by observing the following precautions:

The Farmland Code of Conduct

Farmland is private property and access is only available with the goodwill and tolerance of farmers.

Farmland is a working environment and all persons who enter do so at their own risk. Under the 1995 Occupiers' Liability Act, there is an obligation on entrants to take all necessary steps to ensure their own safety.

Entrants are also responsible for any damage to private property, livestock and crops resulting from their actions. If crossing farmland, ensure your presence is unobtrusive and does not interfere with farming activities.

- Respect farmland and the rural environment.
- Do not interfere with livestock, crops, machinery or other property.
- Guard against all risks of fire especially near forests.
- Leave all farm gates as you find them.
- Always keep children under close control and supervision.
- Avoid entering farmland containing livestock. Your presence can cause stress to livestock and even endanger your safety.
- Do not enter farmland if you have dogs with you, even if on a leash, unless with the permission of the landowner.
- Always use gates, stiles, or other recognised access points and avoid damage to fences, hedges and walls.
- Take all your litter home.
- Take special care on country roads.
- Avoid making any unnecessary noise.
- Protect wildlife, plants and trees.

- Take heed of warning signs – they are there for your protection.
- If following a recognised walking route, keep to the waymarked trail.
- Immediately report any damage caused by your actions to the farmer or landowner.
- Do not block farm entrances when parking.

If you are a member of a sporting or recreational club, please check if you have adequate insurance cover to protect both you and the property owner.

Reproduced courtesy of the IFA.

DO NOT BRING DOGS on any section of the Path which crosses farmland. It crosses fields grazed by cattle and sheep, and any dog seen chasing domestic animals is likely to be shot.

This Path is designed for pilgrims on foot. While some sections on roads or green roads are suitable, sections on paths and especially across bogland are quite unsuitable for horses or mountain bikes, which rapidly create wet, boggy, muddy morasses, that are most unpleasant for all those who follow.

Please do not walk the Path in large groups. Such groups create erosion problems and are seen as intrusive by the occupiers of the land on whose goodwill we depend. They also create problems at stiles or other bottlenecks, often leaving gates open and damaging fences.

5 Disclaimer

To the best of our knowledge the information in this map guide is correct at time of publication, but changes may take place in the route of the Path, which will normally be obvious from the waymarks.

The author, cartographer and publisher accept no responsibility whatever for any loss, damage, or inconvenience sustained or caused as a result of using this map guide, nor for any inaccuracies which there may be.

Landkartenführer für Pilgerwanderwege: Einführung

1 So verwenden Sie den Landkartenführer

Der Text und die Landkarten in diesem Reiseführer richten sich an Wanderer und Pilger, die ihre Wanderung am Hollywood beginnen und zum Gunde lough pilgern.

Der Maßstab ist 1:50.000 (0,5 cm entsprechen 1 km). Alle Landkarten sind nördlich orientiert.

Neben den Landkarten finden Sie eine kurze Beschreibung des auf der Karte angeführten Wegabschnitts. Beim Wandern empfiehlt es sich, die Karte so zu falten, dass die benötigte Seite gezeigt wird, und sie zum Schutz gegen Regen in eine Plastikhülle zu stecken. Weitere Einzelheiten über die verschiedenen Sehenswürdigkeiten entlang des Weges finden Sie nach den Landkarten auf den Seiten.

Natürlich kann in den hier enthaltenen Landkarten nur ein begrenzter Abschnitt der Landschaft entlang der Wanderwege angeführt werden. Wir empfehlen daher, die Vermessungskarten im Maßstab 1:50.000 aus der Reihe Discovery einzupacken, die Ihnen ein vollständiges Bild der Umgebung bieten. Das passende Blatt hierfür ist Nr. 56.

2 Am Weg bleiben

Der Wanderpfad ist durch Wegschilder aus schwarzem, wiederverwertetem Plastik gekennzeichnet, die ein gelbes Pilgersymbol und Pfeile in die jeweilige Wegrichtung aufweisen.
Beim Verlassen der Landstraßen finden Sie ein braunes Schild in Form eines Fingers, auf dem der Name des Wanderwegs und das Pilgersymbol angebracht sind.

3 Sicherheit

Der Wanderweg führt Sie über verkehrsarme und ruhige Landstraßen und Wege, die nur wenige Gefahren in sich bergen. Als Pilger sollten sie jedoch nicht vergessen, dass sich das Wetter schnell ändert und auch geringfügige Verletzungen am Bein zu einem Problem werden können, wenn Sie sich einige

Kilometer von befahrenen Straße befinden. Packen Sie also unbedingt warme Kleidung ein und vergessen Sie nicht wetterfeste Kleidung zum Schutz gegen Regen und Wind. Wanderstiefel sind nicht erforderlich, aber festes Schuhwerk hilft Ihnen beim Meistern unwegiger oder matschiger Pfade. Im unwahrscheinlichen Falle eines Notfalls rufen Sie die Nummer 999. Bedenken Sie bitte, dass Sie beim Wandern auf dem Wanderweg für Ihre eigene Sicherheit verantwortlich sind.

4 Zugang

Auf diesem Wanderweg besteht kein Wegerecht mit Ausnahme der Strecken auf öffentlichen Landstraßen. Abseits dieser Routen überqueren Sie Privatgrundstücke, bei denen Ihnen das Betreten des Grundbesitzes freundlicherweise vom Grundbesitzer gewährt wird. Falls Sie den Bauern beim Ausüben seiner Arbeit behindern, kann er Ihnen das Wegerecht entziehen.

Respektieren Sie also die Großzügigkeit des Grundbesitzers, in dem Sie folgende Vorsichtsmaßnahmen einhalten:

VERHALTENSREGELN AUF DEM LAND

Acker- und Weideland befindet sich im Privatbesitz, den Sie nur aufgrund der Toleranz und Gastfreundschaft des Bauern betreten dürfen.

Es handelt sich um einen Ort, an dem gearbeitet wird, so dass dessen Betretung auf eigene Gefahr erfolgt. Gemäß dem „Occupiers' Liability Act" von 1995 obliegt es demjenigen, der es betritt, alle notwendigen Schritte zur Gewährleistung der eigenen Sicherheit zu unternehmen.

Sie sind auch für sämtliche dem Landbesitz, dem Vieh oder der Feldfrucht zugefügten Schäden haftbar. Beim Überqueren von Acker- und Weideland sollten Sie unbedingt darauf achten, die Aktivitäten des Bauern nicht negativ zu beeinträchtigen.

- Zeigen sie Respekt vor dem Weideland und dem ländlichen Umfeld.
- Machen Sie sich nicht an dem Vieh, der Feldfrucht, Landmaschinen und sonstigem Eigentum zu schaffen.
- Seien Sie sich besonders in Waldgebieten der Gefahr beim Hantieren mit offenem Feuer bewusst.
- Lassen Sie Gatter so, wie Sie sie vorfinden.
- Lassen Sie Kinder nie unbeaufsichtigt.
- Machen Sie einen Bogen um Weideland, auf dem sich Vieh befindet. Ihre

Anwesenheit kann das Vieh beunruhigen und Ihre eigene Sicherheit gefährden.

- Betreten Sie Acker- und Weideland mit einem Hund (auch wenn dieser an der Leine geführt wird) nur mit ausdrücklicher Genehmigung des Grundbesitzers.
- Verwenden Sie nur die zum Zugang vorgesehenen Gatter und Wege und beschädigen Sie keine Zäune, Hecken und Mauern.
- Lassen Sie keine Abfälle liegen.
- Seien Sie auf Landstraßen besonders vorsichtig.
- Machen Sie keinen unnötigen Lärm.
- Schützen sie die Flora und Fauna.
- Beachten Sie jeweils angebrachte Warnschilder; sie dienen zu Ihremeigenen Schutz.
- Wenn Sie sich auf einer anerkannten Wanderroute befinden, gehen Sie nicht davon ab.
- Setzen Sie den Landbesitzer unverzüglich von etwaigen von Ihnen verursachten Schäden in Kenntnis.
- Blockieren Sie nicht die Zufahrten zu den Bauernhöfen.

Wenn Sie Mitglied eines Sport- oder Freizeitvereins sind, vergewissern Sie sich bitte im Voraus, ob Sie über angemessenen Versicherungsschutz verfügen. Damit schützen Sie sowohl sich selbst, als auch den Grundbesitzer.

Reproduziert mit freundlicher Genehmigung des IFA („Irish Farmers Association").

FÜHREN SIE KEINE HUNDE MIT, wenn Sie sich auf einem Wanderweg mit Zugang zu Acker- und Weideland befinden. Sie treffen dabei auf weidende Schafe und Kühe und laufen Gefahr, dass Ihr Hund erschossen wird, wenn er dem Vieh nachjagt.

Dieser Wanderweg ist für Fußmärsche konzipiert. Manche Wegabschnitte sind zwar für Mountain-Bikes oder Pferde geeignet, bestimmte Streckenabschnitte, insbesondere Torfmoore, sind allerdings denkbar ungeeignet dafür. Torfmoore produzieren nämlich einen nassen, sumpfigen und matschigen Morast, auf dem sich ein Ritt oder eine Radfahrt als äußerst schwierig gestalten würde.

Begehen Sie den Wanderweg bitte nicht in großen Gruppen. Dadurch entstehen Erosionsprobleme und es wird auch nicht gern gesehen vom Landbesitzer, auf dessen Gastfreundschaft wir angewiesen sind. Große Gruppen haben an Gattern oder anderen Engpässen Probleme beim Passieren und lassen häufig die Gatter offen bzw. beschädigen die Zäune.

5 Haftungsausschluss

Die Informationen in diesem Landkartenführer sind nach unserem besten Wissen und Gewissen zum Zeitpunkt der Veröffentlichung korrekt. Die Wanderwegroute kann sich jedoch ändern. Derartige Änderungen sind anhand der Wegschilder deutlich gekennzeichnet.

Verfasser, Kartograph und Herausgeber übernehmen keinerlei Verantwortung für etwaige in diesem Landkartenführer enthaltene Ungenauigkeiten bzw. jegliche Verluste, Schäden oder Unannehmlichkeiten, die Ihnen aus der Verwendung dieses Landkartenführers entstehen oder daraus resultieren.

Cartes-Guides Chemins de Pèlerinage: Introduction Génerale

1. Comment utiliser votre carte-guide

Le texte et les cartes contenus dans ce guide sont conçus pour des pèlerins à pied qui partent de Hollywood et terminent leur marche à Glendalough.

Carte à l'échelle du 1: 50.000 (0,5 cm pour 1 kilomètre). Toutes les cartes sont orientées vers le nord.

À côté de chaque carte se trouve une brève description de la section de chemin indiquée sur la carte. Pendant la marche, nous vous suggérons de replier le guide à la page concernée et de le placer dans la pochette plastique qui le protégera des intempéries. Tous renseignements complémentaires concernant les sites intéressants et autres curiosités rencontrés en route se trouvent après les cartes, pages.

Par mesure de nécessité, les cartes de ce guide ne peuvent montrer qu'une section limitée de la région traversée par la voie de pèlerinage. Nous vous conseillons de vous munir des cartes d'État-Major (Ordnance Survey Maps) au 1:50.000 de la série Discovery qui vous donneront une image plus complète de la région. Le feuillet pertinent est le numero 56.

2. Comment reconnaître son chemin

Le chemin est balisé par des panneaux noirs en plastique recyclé, reconnaissables à leur symbole jaune représentant un pèlerin et comportant des flèches qui indiquent la direction à prendre (ces flèches sont adaptées au pèlerin quelle que soit la direction prise).
À l'endroit où le chemin rejoint ou quitte une route publique, se trouve un poteau indicateur marron portant le nom du chemin et le symbole du pèlerin.

3. Sécurité

Cet itinéraire suit des routes tranquilles, des chemins de campagne ou des sentiers et présente très peu de danger. Les pèlerins ne devront pas oublier cependant qu'en Irlande le temps change vite et qu'une blessure même légère à la jambe ou au pied peut poser problème lorsqu'on se trouve à plusieurs kilomètres d'une route publique. Veillez donc à mettre ou à emporter des vêtements chauds et de protection contre la pluie et le vent. Il n'est pas nécessaire de se munir de chaussures de marche, mais portez des chaussures solides et confortables pour franchir les sections boueuses ou accidentées du chemin. Dans l'éventualité très improbable d'un accident nécessitant une aide extérieure, le numéro de téléphone des urgences est le 999. Veuillez noter que vous êtes responsable de votre sécurité personnelle le long de ce chemin.

4 Accès

Ce chemin ne comporte pas de droit de passage à l'exception des sections sur route publique. Ailleurs, il traverse des propriétés privées avec l'aimable autorisation de leurs propriétaires qui pourront en refuser l'accès si les utilisateurs du chemin entravent l'exécution des travaux agricoles ou autres.

Veuillez donc respecter la générosité des propriétaires en observant les règles suivantes :

CODE DE BONNE CONDUITE SUR LES TERRES AGRICOLES

Les terres agricoles sont des propriétés privées et leur accès n'est possible qu'avec le bon vouloir et la tolérance des agriculteurs.

Les terres agricoles représentent un environnement de travail et toute personne qui y pénètre le fait à ses propres risques. La loi "Occupiers' Liability" de 1995 fait obligation aux personnes qui y entrent de prendre toutes mesures nécessaires pour assurer leur sécurité personnelle.

Les personnes qui pénètrent sur des terres agricoles sont également responsables de tous dommages à la propriété de l'agriculteur, son bétail et ses récoltes qui résulteraient de leurs actions. En traversant des terres agricoles, veillez à ce que votre présence soit discrète et n'entravez pas les activités agricoles.

- Respectez les terres agricoles et l'environnement rural.
- Ne touchez jamais au bétail, aux récoltes, aux machines ni à aucun autre bien.
- Prenez toutes précautions contre les risques d'incendie, en particulier à proximité d'une forêt.
- Laissez toutes les barrières d'exploitation agricole dans l'état où vous les trouvez.

- Surveillez toujours de très près les enfants.
- Évitez de pénétrer sur des terres agricoles où se trouve du bétail. Votre présence inquiéterait les animaux et pourrait aussi vous faire courir un danger.
- Ne passez jamais sur des terres agricoles lorsque vous êtes accompagné d'un chien, même en laisse, sauf avec l'autorisation du propriétaire.
- Utilisez toujours les barrières, les échaliers ou autres points d'accès reconnus et évitez d'endommager les clôtures, les haies et les murs.
- Emportez avec vous toutes vos ordures.
- Faites très attention sur les routes de campagne.
- Évitez tout bruit intempestif.
- Protégez la vie sauvage, les plantes et les arbres.
- Respectez les panneaux avertisseurs – ils sont prévus pour votre protection.
- Lorsque vous empruntez un itinéraire de marche reconnu, ne quittez pas le chemin balisé.
- Signalez immédiatement tout dommage résultant de vos actions à l'agriculteur ou au propriétaire.
- Ne bloquez pas les entrées de ferme en garant votre véhicule.

Si vous appartenez à un club sportif ou récréatif, vérifiez que votre assurance est suffisante pour vous protéger, vous-même et le propriétaire.

Reproduit avec l'aimable autorisation de l'IFA.

NE VENEZ PAS AVEC UN CHIEN sur les sections du chemin qui traversent des terres agricoles. Ces sections passent en effet par des prés occupés par du bétail et des moutons, et les chiens que l'on voit pourchasser des animaux domestiques sont généralement abattus.

Ce chemin est destiné aux pèlerins à pied. Même si certaines sections sur route ou route verte leur conviennent, d'autres sections de l'itinéraire, en particulier dans les tourbières, sont totalement inadaptées aux VTT et aux chevaux qui les transforment rapidement en un marécage humide, spongieux et boueux, tout à fait désagréable pour ceux qui suivent.

Ne faites pas cette marche en groupes trop nombreux. Ces groupes créent un problème d'érosion et sont considérés comme gênants par les occupants des terres dont le bon vouloir nous est indispensable. Ils créent également des problèmes au niveau des échaliers ou autres goulets d'étranglement, et laissent souvent des barrières ouvertes et endommagent des clôtures.

5 Clause de non responsabilité

À notre connaissance, les informations contenues dans cette carte-guide sont exactes au moment de la mise sous presse. Il pourra cependant se produire des modifications dans le tracé du chemin qui seront normalement indiquées de manière évidente par la signalisation.

L'auteur, le cartographe et l'éditeur ne pourront en aucun cas être tenus responsables de pertes ou de dommages subis quels qu'ils soient ou de désagréments causés en conséquence de l'utilisation de cette carte-guide, ou d'inexactitudes éventuelles.

Useful phone numbers and addresses
Nützliche Adressen
Adresses utiles

EMERGENCY SERVICE - Telephone 999 or 122
Coastal, Mountain, and Cave Rescue, Fire, Gardaí, Ambulance, Lifeboat

WICKLOW TOURISM OFFICE	**(0404) 69117**
GLENDALOUGH (SEASONAL)	**(0404) 45688**
WICKLOW MOUNTAINS NATIONAL PARK, Information point	**(0404) 45425**

IARNRÓD EIREANN –
(Rail Passenger information)
(01) 8366222
www.irishrail.ie

BUS EIREANN –
(Passenger information)
(01) 836 6111
www.buseireann.ie

AN ÓIGE –
(Irish Youth Hostel Association)
(01) 830 4555
Fax: 01 830 5808
www.anoige.ie

INDEPENDENT HOLIDAY HOSTELS –
(01) 836 4700
Fax: 01 836 4710

THE PILGRIM PATHS PROJECT

In 1997 the Pilgrims Paths project was set up by the Heritage Council. The objective of this project is to develop and support a network of walking routes along medieval Pilgrim Paths in association with local communities. The aim of the project is to raise awareness of the different aspects of heritage, built and natural, encountered along the routes while contributing to sustainable tourism and community development in each local area.

The routes included in the project are:

1. COSÁN NA NAOMH - on the Dingle Peninsula, Co Kerry
2. ST. KEVIN'S WAY from Hollywood to Glendalough, Co Wicklow
3. LOUGH DERG - a route to the shore opposite Saints Island, Co Donegal
4. SLÍ MHÓR - Ballycumber/Leamonaghan to Clonmacnois, Co Offaly
5. ST. DECLAN'S WAY from Lismore to Ardmore

The Heritage Council gratefully acknowledges the work of the local routes committees whose dedication to the project is vital to its success.

This project has been supported by the Pilot Tourism and Environment Scheme 1999 (Bord Fáilte Eireann) and the National Millennium Committee.

I. Historical Background

St. Kevin's Road is a walk of about 18 miles/30 kilometers which has two alternative starting points, reflecting the different directions from which pilgrims to Glendalough are likely to have come during the medieval period, before joining up together to reach Saint Kevin's resting place in the heart of the Wicklow Hills. Though it does not always slavishly follow the ancient route in its entirety, the road reflects the original way that Kevin followed in his search for a mountain hermitage where he could communicate in peace with his Maker.

St. Kevin belonged to a once-influential family, the Dál Messe Corb which, at the dawn of Irish history, had land in the fertile valley of the river Liffey to the west of the mountains. It was presumably somewhere there that St. Kevin was born in the sixth century, and tradition locates his birth-place at Tipperkevin, two miles from Ballymore Eustace, where a well (in Irish Tobar Chaoimhín) still manifests his cult. After initial training at Kilnamanagh (Cell na Manach – the Monks Cell) near Tallaght, at the northern foot of the Dublin/Wicklow hills, he then walked across them until he found his resting place at Glendalough (Gleann da locha – the Glen of Two Lakes). There he stayed, and spent the rest of his life in solitary contemplation and prayer amid the spiritual surroundings of the valley which, in the words of Michael Rodgers and Marcus Losack, 'expresses its beautiness and holiness through many different moods; sometimes sombre, sometimes sunny, always haunting and mysterious'. But, after his death in 618, what had been his humble hermit's retreat developed into an impressive monastic city which was to continue its active life as a centre of piety and learning for many centuries to come.

The saint's reputation for sanctity spread to such an extent that pilgrims both lay and ecclesiastical came from far and wide to venerate his relics – The Annals of the Four Masters recording, for instance, the deaths at Glendalough of Daighre Ua Dubhatan, anmchara ('soul-friend') of Clonmacnois in 1056, and Ceannfaeladh, abbot of Seir Kieran (also in County Offaly) in 951 – the first person who is documented as having 'died on his pilgrimage to Gleann-da-locha'. At that stage, the Viking city of Dublin was only just beginning to expand, and it is its present-day inhabitants who make up the largest proportion of those who visit Glendalough today, travelling through the village of Laragh to approach the valley from the east. But, in medieval times, the majority would have approached it from the opposite direction, coming from the fertile midlands to the west of the mountain massif. For those plains people of Ireland, going on pilgrimage to Glendalough would have entailed the penitential discomfort of clambering up unaccustomed hillsides through virtually uninhabited territory in order to come closer to the holiness and relics of the saint, and to aspire to a higher place in heaven. Such pilgrims have left no literary record of their experiences, of what they did, what prayers they said, nor, with very few exceptions such as those quoted above, even where they came from. Some may have started their journey from St. Brigid's town of Kildare – another important centre of pilgrimage – and commenced their trek across the hills from somewhere near Valleymount, where our Alternative Route starts (see p.26). However, most are likely to have foregathered at Hollywood, where our main walk begins.

From here, the journey involves walking in what, on the whole, are comparatively easy stages towards the Wicklow gap which is over 1500 feet/450 metres above sea level, before following the descent of the Glendasan river into the Valley of Glendalough itself. Because parts of the track have been overgrown, or otherwise obliterated, it is not always possible to follow the road's original course, but ancient traces including placenames combined with common sense, together with a desire to avoid busy road traffic wherever possible for safety reasons, and acquiescence in the understandable wishes of local landowners, have dictated the choice of route followed here.

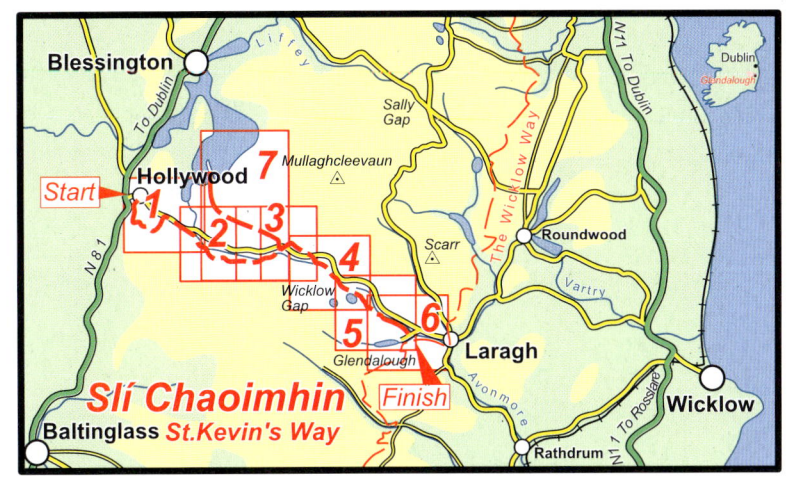

KEY TO MAP SYMBOLS

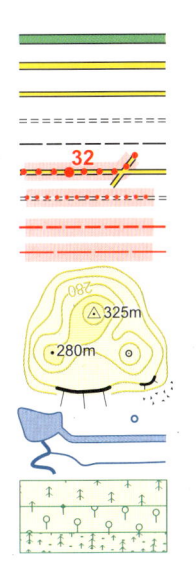

- National Main Road
- Main Road
- Minor Road
- Dirt/ Gravel Road
- Footpath
- Following a Road
- Following a Dirt Road
- Following a Footpath
- No Path or Indistinct
- Contour Lines (20m)
- Trigonometric Pillar
- Spot Height, Cairn
- Cliff
- Rocky Terrain
- Lake/ Well/ Water Tap
- Large River
- River, Stream
- Forest - Coniferous
- Forest - Deciduous
- Felled/ New Plantation

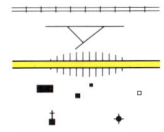

- Railway
- Wall/ Fence
- Village/ Houses
- Building, Ruin
- Church, Mast

The route of the St. Kevin's Way is shown in RED. Distances are marked by a red dot every kilometre, going from Hollywood to Glendalough.

- Shop, Pub, Post Office
- Phone, Cafe, Craft Shop
- Petrol, Bureau de Change
- Tourist Office, Doctor
- Parking, Picnic Site, Bus
- Hotel, Bed & Breakfast
- Hostel, Caravan/ Campsite
- Site of Interest, Museum
- Rath, Castle, Church
- Tomb, Barrow, Fulacht Fia
- Golf, Traditional Music
- Horse Riding, Fishing

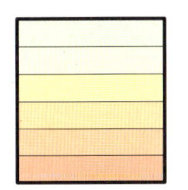

- Relief - 100 to 200 metres
- Relief - 200 to 300 metres
- Relief - 300 to 400 metres
- Relief - 400 to 500 metres
- Relief - 500 to 600 metres
- Relief - 600 metres +

Map Scale 1:50000

0 Km — 1 Km — 2 Km — 3 Km — 4 Km — 5 Km

The representation on this map of any road, track or path is no evidence of the existence of a right of way

II. Main Route Start From Hollywood
Hollywood to Coonmore, km 0-8

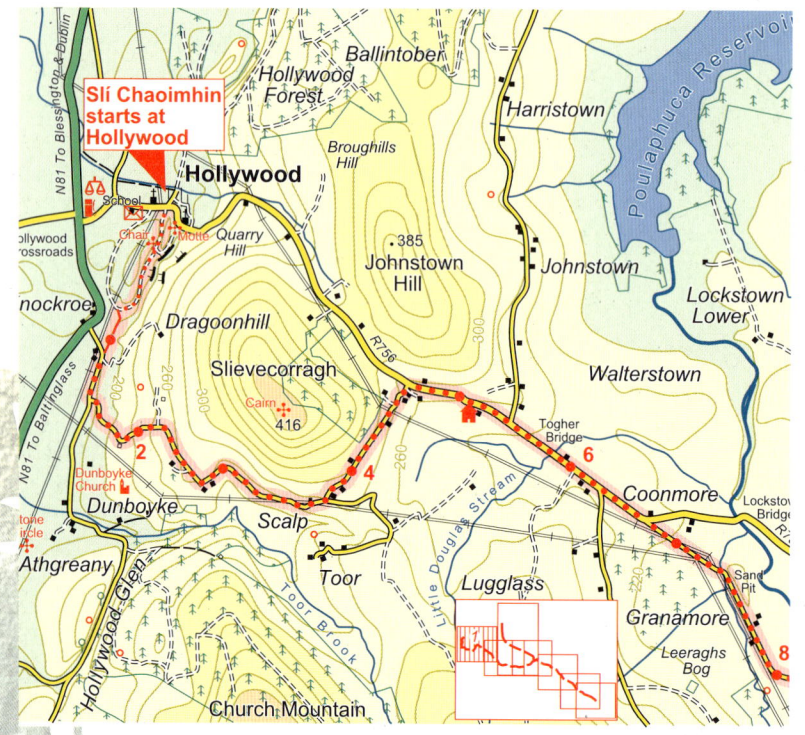

Hollywood, just off the busy road from Baltinglass to Blessington, is the starting point for the main route of St. Kevin's Road. Much more populous before the Great Famine of the mid-nineteenth century – the parish numbers dropped from 2770 in 1841 to 366 in 1966 – the village, being a cul-de-sac, has been able to retain its rural simplicity through an unspoiled architecture of pub, dwellings and converted forge with horseshoe-shaped entrance. The factual history of Hollywood goes half-way back to the time of St. Kevin, as the motte-and-bailey in Knockroe townland near the village is a reminder that this was a Norman borough from as early as the thirteenth century. At that stage, its name was recorded as 'Holy Wood', a translation of the Latin description *Sanctum Nemus* used in an Irish Life of St. Kevin written some thousand years ago. This biography tells of how an angel opened up a path in the wood to enable the saint to reach Glendalough, perhaps echoing some old tradition that it was the saint's followers who caused the track across the mountains to start from here, rather than from the prehistoric stone circle at Athgreany known as 'The Piper's Stones'.

A few hundred metres uphill from the village on the tarmacadamed road to Glendalough is what must surely have been the assembly-point for pilgrims in days gone by – the old church of St. Kevin which, though usually closed, is very occasionally used by the Church of Ireland for divine service, or for community purposes. Built perhaps around 1700 with an unusual barrel-vaulted ceiling, the church stands on raised ground, suggesting centuries of earlier use that is confirmed by the presence of two medieval cross-decorated stones in the churchyard. In addition, and age-old holy well dedicated to St. Kevin is located not far outside the purlieus of the church, to the north-west.

Just where the village street veers off at an angle from the Wicklow Gap/Glendalough road, the start of our pilgrimage path is marked by a signpost pointing southwards towards Knockroe (Cnoc Ruadh – 'red hill'). This is a spectacular gorge carved out by water escaping southwards from the Glacial Lake Blessington (formed 22,000 – 14,000 years ago) along a major fault separating sandstones to the west, from the shales and schists interbedded with basaltic lava to the east. Nowadays, its slopes are overgrown with bracken and gorse, resounding at times to the song of the linnet, the greenfinch and the stonechat. The ornithologist might even be lucky enough to encounter the occasional peregrine here. The Norman motte-and-bailey dominates the glen on the left and, farther along the path on the right (roughly opposite were a small 1913 statue of St. Kevin stands on the cliff-top), there is a stone known as St. Kevin's Chair, marked with a double-armed cross of uncertain age and said to be beneficial in curing back-ache. Not far away is an old tree reputed to have been one of the 'stations' where pilgrims stopped to say a prayer.

St.Kevin's Church,Hollywood

Continuing along the glen which was doubtless an ancient thoroughfare, we cross a stile out onto a country road for a short distance before turning left up a fairly steep hill along the Scalp road. From here, a good view can be had of a church site at Dunboyke (Dún Buchat), visible about half a mile across a valley on the right, and located just next to a tall electricity pylon. In its present ruined state, it is a late medieval nave-and-chancel structure preserving and old rotary quern and a bullaun (see p. 38) which suggest that pilgrims may have diverted from the

The Kings River valley

main route during the Middle Ages to stop and say a prayer here. Also visible on the right from farther along on the Scalp road is the Jackdaws Glen (Gleann na gCág in Irish) where the archaeologically-trained eye will detect a rath or ring-fort (with partially-preserved second bank) located on a slope close to a farm barn on the opposite side of the valley. Such raths, now empty within, once contained houses built by affluent farmers around 500-1000 A.D. as their family residence, surrounded by the circular bank to protect their cattle from human and animal predators. At Dunbolg, somewhere nearby, a famous battle full of stratagems was fought in the year 598, in which the Leinstermen defeated the invading army of the king of Ulster and decapitated him.

At about the 3.5 kilometre mark on the map, the road straight ahead may approximate more closely to the line of the old St. Kevin's Road but, because it gets lost in low-lying terrain, we turn left instead along the south-eastern slope of Slievecorragh to join up with the country road R 756 from Hollywood to Glendalough. But beware:

This is the most dangerous part of the whole route, as cars and motorcycles drive along this 2km stretch of road far too fast!
Keep on the right-hand side of the road and walk against the traffic-flow.

About half-way along, the road dips to cross over the Little Douglas Stream at Togher Bridge – a significant name, as the Irish word Tóchar has been used since time immemorial to denote a causeway or roadway, made sometimes of wood.

At Coonmore (meaning in Irish 'the big bend'), the main road to the Wicklow Gap (R 756) takes a left turn towards and over Lockstown Bridge (not far from where the famous labyrinth stone p.36 was found), through Granabeg and on to Ballinagee Bridge, where it is joined by our Alternative Route coming from Valleymount (p.26), and which is also the goal of the road where we go straight ahead at Coonmore. Parts of the R 756 on the opposite (northern) bank of the Kings River are usually taken to reflect the line of the old St. Kevin's Road, but there are some who would argue that our, more direct, road from Coonmore to Ballinagee Bridge, close to the river's southern bank, has an equally valid claim.

Shortly after we go straight ahead at Coonmore fork, the road crosses a tributary of the Kings River over an attractive granite bridge bearing the date 1875.

Just beyond it, at Granamore, is a sand pit, where both sand and gravel were deposited as a delta by a river flowing into the Ice-Age glacial Lake Blessington. A thin layer of peat near the top of the deposit was disrupted by ice moving over it before more sand and gravel were laid above it. The same deposits also surface farther along to the left between road and river, at the 8 km mark on the map, in the form of tongues of higher ground covered with bracken and grass which wedge out into the boggy areas to the west. In contrast, the opposite bank at the 10 km mark had bands of coarse-grained peaty sand alternating with finer white sand.

Leeraghs bog on the hillside to the south of our road, and located at the centre left of map 2, is one of the few examples of a raised bog in County Wicklow, where most of the hills are otherwise covered in blanket bog. Its slightly domed shape comes from its having formed in a shallow basin. Its peat is, on average, about 2-3 metres deep, whereas the blanket bog elsewhere in the area often has a depth of only about one metre.

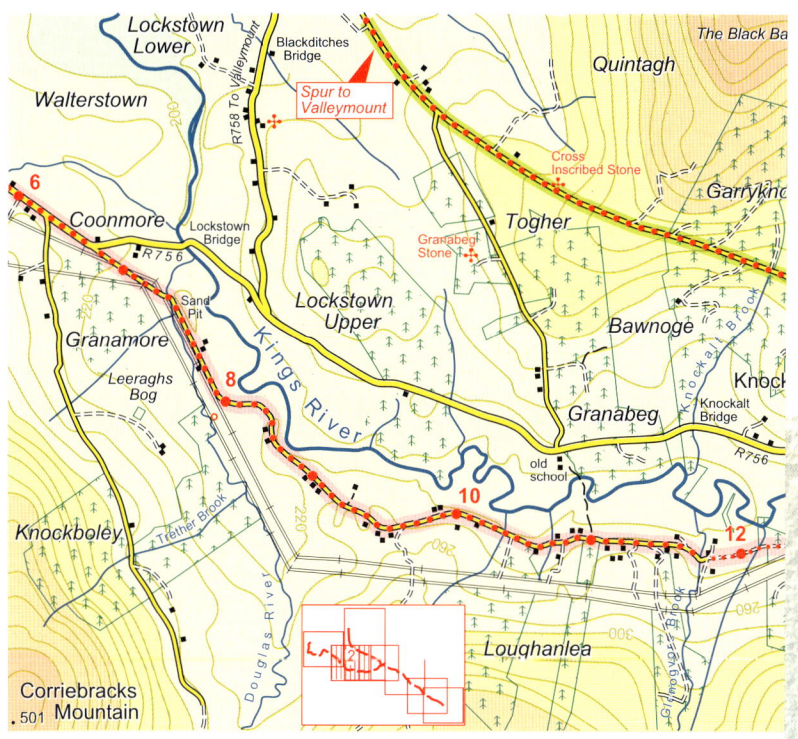

From Coonmore, Km 6-12

The more than 7 km stretch from Coonmore to Ballinagee Bridge sees our road playing games with the south bank of the Kings River, now closing in on it, now distancing itself, as its waters flow meanderingly through clean, flat fields in the opposite direction. The area may have had a sacred character in prehistoric times, as we encounter placenames such as Knock-na-Droose (Cnoc na Druaithe), the hill of the Druids, who may well have conducted their rituals in an oakwood, represented by the placename Coill Doire. But this is also Wicklow sheep country *par excellence*, where domestic duck can also be seen to provide small variety in the animal world. One of the strongest features of the landscape hereabouts is the presence of granite in many shapes and sizes. Some very large boulders litter the fields as erratic leftovers from the Ice-Age glaciers, while smaller examples, sparkling with mica when not embraced by soft and gentle moss, have been used to construct remarkable stone walls that divide up pastures and reflect age-old land divisions. Others have been used to great effect in building houses, including one particularly notable structure with its gable-end on to the road. The peace and tranquillity sensed along this stretch of the route gives the walker the satisfaction of being able to avoid the hassle of traffic on the main road running along the opposite side of the valley.

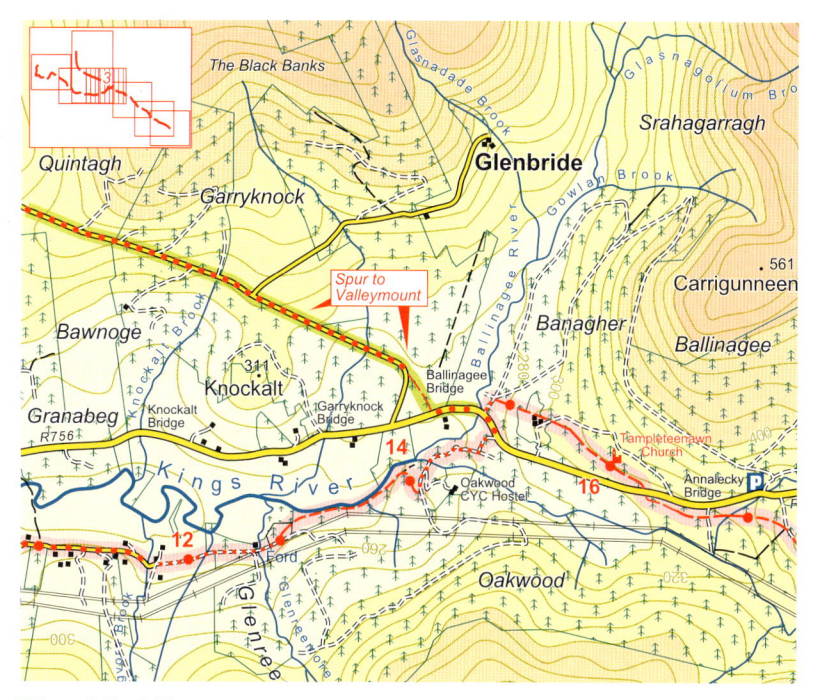

Km 12-17 to beyond Annalecky Bridge

Passing through a gateway at the end of the actual road, we walk along a path for a short distance before coming to a set of stepping stones over the Glenreemore Brook which, if in spate, can be crossed by a nearby bridge. It was at the head of this rivulet that Art O'Neill died while taking shelter with Red Hugh O'Donnell after they had escaped from Dublin Castle and were heading for the parallel valley of Glenmalure to the south in the bitterly-cold Christmas of 1592. In 1932, a wooden cross was erected on the mountain above the place where tradition says he perished.

Shortly after the stepping stones, we turn left into a former plantation, long established but recently felled, before entering a wooded area, along a path still bearing the name of 'The Gentlemen's Way'. With the soothing sound of the moving waters of the Kings River on the left, this is one of the most pleasing and romantic stretches of the whole walk. Emerging from the brief sylvan interlude, we approach an old ford, above which we cross a recent bridge over the river and climb gently along a path before finally re-joining once more the bustling R 756 from Hollywood to Glendalough. Unexpectedly, we turn left, as if re-tracing our steps towards Hollywood, but only for a few hundred metres before crossing the road (again watch out for fast traffic!) and turning into a short laneway on the right.

Because this is where the Alternative Route joins us, we should now interrupt our narrative to go to Valleymount where it starts, and then follow its course until it catches up with us at Ballinagee Bridge.

The Alternative Route – over 7 km

The Alternative Route starts in the small village of Valleymount, anciently, and doubtless significantly, called An Chrois ('The Cross'), an indication that it was formerly on church lands. It could even have been an assembly point for pilgrims coming along the upper Liffey Valley from St. Brigid's sanctuary at Kildare, who may have detoured earlier to visit St. Kevin's traditional birthplace at Tipperkevin (p.17) before proceeding on their way across the hills to Glendalough. An attractive cross bearing the dates 1846, 1875 and 1938, stands outside the village church housing interesting stained glass of the 1930s. Like so many buildings in the locality, it relies heavily on the use of well-hewn granite from the quarries at Ballyknockan nearby. Its most notable and unexpected feature is the façade with Spanish colonial echoes, said to have been inspired by returning emigrant miners who had been working in Mexico. The original landscape in the vicinity was totally altered from its medieval appearance when the Kings River valley was partially flooded to create a large reservoir around 1940.

The Alternative Route is over 7km from Valleymount to Ballinagee Bridge, where it joins up with the main route that started at Hollywood. Where the walk begins to climb, just over one kilometre south of Valleymount, we do not take the road to the right that leads to Lockstown Upper, where the famous labyrinth stone (p.36) was found in 1908, though it is no longer in situ, as it is on display in the National Museum in Dublin. Instead, we continue on straight up the hill to Togher, where a right-hand fork down an untarred lane would bring you past a quarry on your left and an abandoned cottage on your right, immediately after which a path leads down 250 paces through the forest to the Granabeg stone, which has a cross standing out in relief on one face. It stands on an angular pile of stones which may indicate the former presence of a pilgrim path there, further traces of which may be found in the field-clearing beyond.

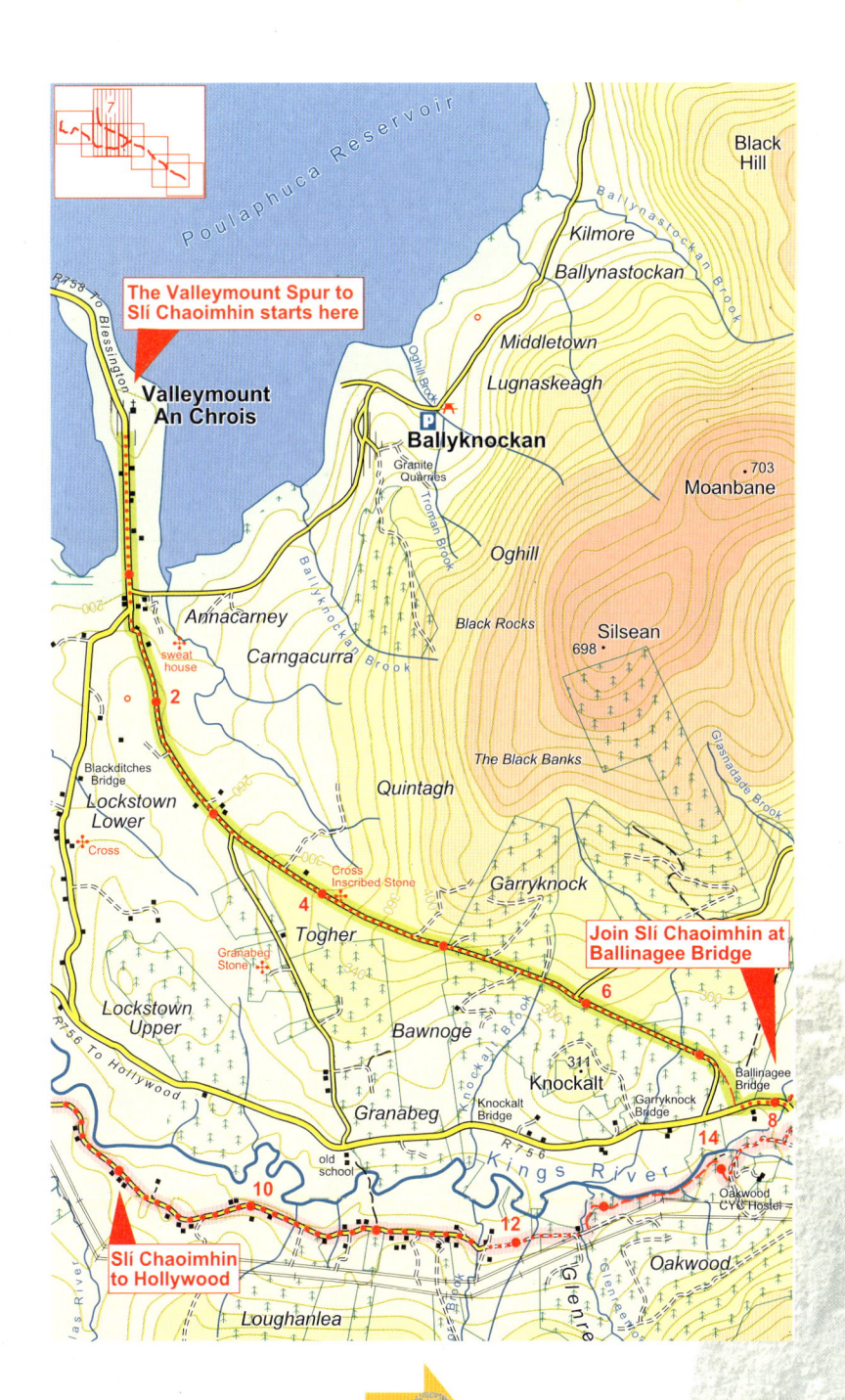

Poulaphuca Reservoir

Black Hill

Ballynastockan Brook

Kilmore

Ballynastockan

R758 To Blessington

The Valleymount Spur to Slí Chaoimhin starts here

Middletown

Lugnaskeagh

Oghill Brook

Valleymount An Chrois

Ballyknockan

Granite Quarries

.703
Moanbane

Ballyknockan Brook

Annacarney

Carngacurra

Oghill

sweat house

Black Rocks

Silsean
698

2

Glasnadade Brook

Blackditches Bridge

Lockstown Lower

The Black Banks

Cross

Quintagh

Garryknock

Cross Inscribed Stone

4

Togher

Join Slí Chaoimhin at Ballinagee Bridge

Granabeg Stone

Lockstown Upper

6

R756 To Hollywood

Bawnoge

311

Knockalt

Ballinagee Bridge

Granabeg

Knockalt Bridge

Garryknock Bridge

14

8

Kings River

old school

10

Oakwood CYC Hostel

Slí Chaoimhin to Hollywood

12

Oakwood

Loughanlea

Glenreemore Brook

27

But, rather than being distracted by that by-way, our route continues on straight uphill at Togher. Approaching the brow of the hill just over four kilometres from Valleymount, and some two hundred paces beyond a solitary bush on the left, there is a low boulder, in the grassy bank beside the road with a cross, which could have been carved into it a thousand years ago or more. It was the antiquarian Liam Price who was the first to establish the link between this stone and St. Kevin's Road in a 1940 article (see bibliography, p.40) which remains the most important work ever written on our pilgrimage path. A glance over the left shoulder from this cross-inscribed stone provides a splendid view of the sixty-year old Poulaphuca reservoir. Continuing our route, the road begins to lead downhill through a forestry plantation with an abandoned village. Emerging from the trees, the walker gets a first sight of the Wicklow Gap, with the straight and smoothened rim of the electricity reservoir on the horizon at the top of Turlough Hill (see p.38). Our path goes then in a direct line to a gate giving on to the dangerous R 756, where the cross erected to the memory of Art O'Neill (p. 25) can be seen on the sky-line above the Kings River. Turning briefly to the left along the road, we turn into a laneway, also on the left, which is where we join the main route coming from Hollywood and approaching us, unexpectedly, from the opposite direction. Having entered the forestry plantation just to the east of Ballinagee Bridge, go over the stile provided to the right, continue straight for a short while before turning right up a hill and along a path provided by Coillte, the Forestry Service, that runs above and roughly parallel to the R 756.

Resting at Annalecky Bridge.

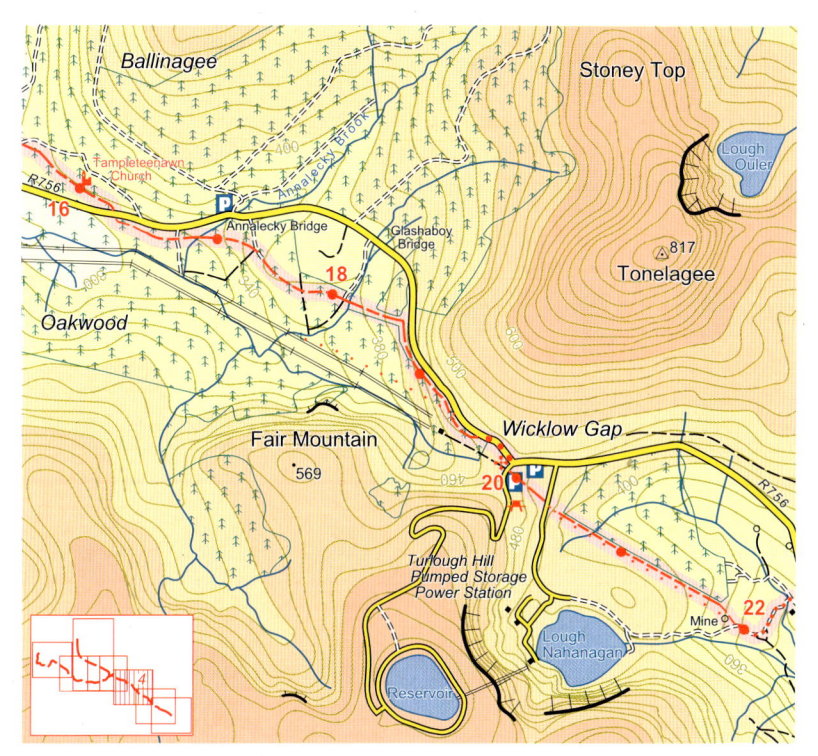

BALLINAGEE BRIDGE TO THE WICKLOW GAP AND LOUGH NAHANAGAN KM 16-22

At kilometre-mark 16 on the map, we encounter Tampleteenawn, a church with little more than its foundations remaining, but with a narrow nave-and-chancel plan and south doorway that could suggest a construction date in the twelfth or, at latest, the thirteenth century. However, references as late as 1530 associating it with Sir Galfridus Harold, who lived in the mountains, could suggest that it continued in use at least until the Reformation. Liam Price has suggested that the name was originally tempull tighe Fhionáin ('the church of the house of Finan'), the Finan being perhaps the holy man of that name from North Leinster who is reported to have been cured of an illness in Kildare, which could be another pointer linking the Glendalough pilgrimage with St. Brigid's city.

Continuing on through a gate and over a stile, our walk crosses the R 756 once again **(Danger from Speeding Traffic)**, and continues on inside the fence on the south side of the road before reaching an extensive section of woodland near Annalecky Bridge – the Irish words Abhann na Leice meaning 'the river of the flat stones'. We cross one new wooden bridge near the entrance, and another shortly afterwards, as well as jumping across one very small stream, before a gradual ascent takes us upwards to a right-hand turn after which we rejoin the R 756 for the final kilometre before reaching the Wicklow Gap. The geologist Adrian Phillips has this to say about the side of Fair Mountain that we see to the right before reaching the Gap:

> 'The dark crags to the south of the path are formed by two bands of schist within the granite which forms paler, more rounded, crags. The continuation of these bands can be seen in small crags above the road just to the west of the Wicklow Gap. The schist bands are displaced about 300m to the right across the Wicklow Gap. This is evidence that the valley here, and on to Glendalough, has been formed by erosion along a WNW-trending fault which offset the rocks on either side. Above the road, just west of the Gap, there is a small quarry with hummocks of granite surrounded by a white sandy material consisting of rotted granite. This is a fine example of the sort of deep chemical weathering which requires a hot semi-arid climate of the sort which existed in Ireland during the Tertiary period 60-20 million years ago.

The Wicklow Gap, a classic example of a 'wind gap', is the highest point reached by the walker, forming a saddle between Tonelegee and Turlough Hill. On the right, the side-road leading off the R 756 towards the Electricity Supply Board's reservoir at the top of the latter (see p.38) is flanked on either side by a small rectangular fenced-off area directly adjoining the car park. Raised more than a metre above the present ground level, these areas contain the best visible examples of the old Pilgrimage Road, consisting of remnants of the original irregular paving stones creating a path more

Original flagsotnes of the old Pilgrim's road at the Wicklow gap

than three metres wide (for more details see p.37), and to the east and west of these enclosures further raised stretches of the road can be seen. The small rock crags on the hillside to the south are formed of granite, elongated East-West with smooth surfaces on their eastern end and with jagged western ends, a circumstance caused by ice flowing smoothly up from the east over the crags and carrying bits of rock off from the downstream western ends. Lough Nahanagan at the foot of the cliffs was where a small valley glacier formed and flowed eastwards down the Vale of Glendasan between 11,000 and 10,000 years ago. The high ridge in front of the lake that acts as a natural dam for its waters is a terminal moraine, formed of debris washed out from the snout of the glacier just before it finally melted.

Whereas the present main road (R 756) descends eastwards from the Gap in a wide semi-circle cradled in the contours of Tonelegee and Brockagh mountains, and where drainage works recently exposed fossil pines that had grown there extensively between 7000 and 4000 years ago, the old Pilgrim Path continues straight on, across the modern ESB road leading to Lough Nahanagan, and follows the southern end of a forestry plantation for about 2 kilometers. The line of the old pilgrimage road, on the other side of the fence to our right, was discovered some decades ago by the late Paddy Healy, who plotted the path of the paving stones by putting down metal rods through a metre or more of the peat which overlay them. Our route, recently laid bare for walkers, displays occasional granite boulders, still remarkable for their whiteness before they take on the weathered patina to which we are more accustomed. The surrounding bog is an excellent example of blanket peatland, where species of purple moor-grass, deer sedge and heath rush are found. More common are the ling and bell heather, which can be robust and tall due to low grazing pressure from sheep and deer, though red deer droppings do betray their presence in the area. On the hillside to the south of the bog, the bedrock changes to a granite that was intruded as a hot liquid around 400 million years ago. The crags above the valley show mica-schist (andalusite bearing) with south-east inclined layering that was laid down as horizontal layers of deep-sea mud and silt some 90 million years earlier. They were subsequently converted to schist by the underlying intrusion of the hot molten granite already mentioned, and folded during the collision of the south-east and north-west of Ireland.

LEAD MINES TO GLENDALOUGH KM 22-26

Near where our route crosses a new footbridge before briefly rejoining the R 756 close to the 23 km mark on the map, buildings associated with lead-mining activity around the 1830s come into view on the right (for more about which, see p.39). Below the mine buildings, we leave the R 756 for the last time, making a fairly steep descent between yellow-blooming gorse and splendid granite boulders, crossing an old spoil-heap so full of acid that nothing grows on it, dropping down past another mining building, and crossing the Glendasan river to walk along the valley floor for the remainder of the walk. The sides of this lower part of the valley show that fields intensively grazed little more than half a century ago are now covered in gorse scrub, reflecting a declining rural population.

Anthills provide evidence for the antiquity of the grazed lands. Skaters, dippers and grey wagtails, as well as sika deer, are frequently visible in the open woodlands on the north side of the valley. That may well be the side upon which the pilgrims walked, but our path brings us along the southern bank of the Glendasan river, past St. Kevin's and St. Lorcan's retreat houses, and keeping some old-looking stepping stones to our left farther on before trees join the path beside the river. Just beyond a weir, our route turns slightly to the right near St. Kevin's Keeve and suddenly the Round Tower of the old monastery looms up ahead of us. We have finally arrived at the pilgrims' goal of Glendalough.

Pilgrim walkers at the head of the Glendasan valley

THE OLD MONASTERY AT GLENDALOUGH

As mentioned earlier, the old monastery grew up around the tomb of the hermit Saint Kevin after his death in 618 and, in time, it became a centre of piety, pilgrimage and learning. Yet little survives from the first three centuries of its existence, because churches and monks' houses would have been built largely of wood, which fell a prey to fire and decay. The Cathedral may be the only surviving building to be older than the year 1000, and most of the others are likely to date from the eleventh and twelfth centuries - perhaps the greatest era of pilgrimage that Europe has ever seen.

But before even setting foot on old monastic terrain, the walker would be well advised to pay a visit to the Interpretative Centre beside the car park, where something of the valley's historical background can be gleaned, and where there is a model showing the monastery as it would have been in its heyday. But then return to the roadbridge beside the hotel, because under that bridge can still be seen some of the old stepping stones which pilgrims would have used to cross the Glendasan River before the bridge was built less than two hundred years ago.

Having reached dry land, the pilgrim would have walked up through the medieval double-arched entrance, the only such monastic gateway to survive anywhere in Ireland. After emerging from the second arch, the visitor who has now entered the old monastic sanctuary is greeted by a large cross carved on a boulder on the right-hand side. Further along to the right is the Round Tower, restored in 1876 and one of the best preserved examples in the country, reaching a height of about 100 feet. It may once have acted as the monastic treasury but, being so tall, it would also have beckoned to pilgrims from afar, to show where their goal lay and give them strength to complete the last few miles of their journey.

George Campbell's Glendalough

Close by is the Cathedral, the second largest pre-Norman church in the country. Started perhaps in the tenth century, and seemingly using some parts of an earlier building, it had a chancel added late in the twelfth century. Passing among some quaint old tombstones, and a medieval granite cross, a path leads to St. Kevin's church, also known as St. Kevin's kitchen because the small Round Tower emerging from its roof reminded people of a kitchen chimney. Glendalough's most characteristic building, and dating probably from the twelfth century, it is one of the few churches in Ireland that have been roofed entirely in stone.

A nearby stile leads to a ruined church on the left dedicated to St. Ciarán, the founder of a great Irish monastery at Clonmacnois, the goal of another of our pilgrim walks. It marks the end of the main core of the monastic settlement at Glendalough, but the valley has plenty more of interest to offer. The path leads across a bridge to a T-junction, marked by a bullaun stone known as the Deer Stone where, according to tradition, the deer offered milk to St. Kevin. To the left, a path leads down the southern side of the valley to the Romanesque priory church of St. Saviour, difficult to find among the trees, and often associated with Glendalough's second saint, Laurence O'Toole, who was canonised in 1226. But the path to the right at the Deer Stone leads after a mile or so to the upper part of the valley where, above a lovely glacial lake often flanked with gorse, the church of Reefert can be seen, within whose walls sleep many Leinster kings. Close by, but very dangerous of access, is St. Kevin's Bed, a man-made cavity in a steep rock-face where the saint is said to have lived, and to have been tempted by a young lady enamoured of his looks and who he finally, in frustration, threw headlong into the cold lake waters below, at least according to a famous ballad by Thomas Moore!

A path on the far side of the valley brings the walker as far as he or she can go with ease, up to the old leadmines at the head of the valley, where some of the old buildings and spoil-heaps can still be seen today. The mines would have largely gone out of production by 1862, the year when the Catholic church closed down the Glendalough pilgrimage because it had become too much of a fun-fair as pictured so vividly in Peacock's painting of fifty years earlier (p.34).

Peacock's painting of Glendalough in 1813 shows how the pilgrimage had turned into a colourful annu

the saint's feastday.

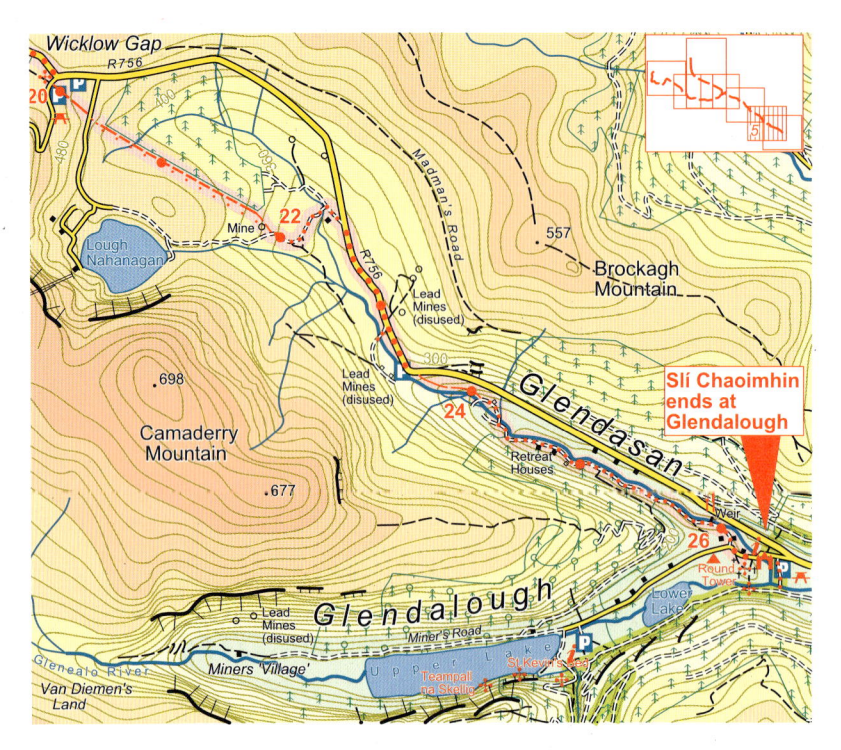

THE HOLLYWOOD LABYRINTH STONE

When a large granite boulder was upturned during a stoat chase in the townland of Lockstown Upper in 1908, it was found to have a labyrinth design carved on one face. The stone lay on a rock-strewn grassy lane not far from the Pilgrims' Road, and between the Main and the Alternative Route described here. Because of the rarity of the design in ancient Ireland, the stone was transported in the 1930s to the National Museum in Dublin, where it is now prominently displayed in the central court. Though Egyptian in origin, the labyrinth is usually seen as the one designed by Daedalus for King Minos in Crete, and associated with the legend of Theseus and Ariadne. For

36

Christians it had various meanings, including the path of life, with a broad entrance leading through difficult passages to an exit, which they believed could only be reached with the help of Christ. Though some good parallels for this Irish labyrinth are found in prehistoric contexts elsewhere, the stone's location so close to St. Kevin's Road could make it more amenable to a symbolic interpretation for the pilgrim as a way to transverse the road of a Christian life. The forty-foot wide example laid on the floor of Chartres Cathedral, where pilgrims negotiated the twists and turns on their knees, has often been taken as a substitute for going on pilgrimage to Jerusalem, though there seems to be no medieval documentation for this tradition. Even so, the Hollywood stone may also have some similar connotation.

The Pilgrims' Road – The Tóchar

In 1972, the National Museum of Ireland carried out an excavation on sections of the old St. Kevin's Road at the top of the Wicklow Gap, just beside the junction of the R756 with the Electricity Supply Board's private road leading up to its reservoir on the summit of Turlough Hill. A wooden fence encloses each of the surviving excavated sections of the Pilgrimage Road – the only one of its kind to have been examined scientifically in Ireland. Prior to the excavation, the road had been covered at this point with 15cm of peat, though elsewhere the peat cover reached depths of 1.5m. The road proved to have been built of roughly rectangular granite slabs, some resting directly on the bog surface, others on smaller stones beneath them, but never with any clear indication that there was a man-made substratum to support them. The pavement, sometimes with a low bank on one or both sides, was reasonably level, but the gaps between stones would have rendered the road impractical for wheeled vehicles. Even horses would have found the going difficult, though there would have been ample room for them, as the road was more than 3m wide. A metal token, probably of seventeenth-century date, was found in a small depression in the paving during excavation, but that only proved that the road was still in use three hundred years ago, and did not date the road itself. Sometime between the eighth and the twelfth century is the most likely period for the construction of the road, but this remains nothing more than a guess in the absence of any finds to prove it. It has been estimated that if 25 men worked six days a week for eight months of the year, it could have taken them up to twenty years to build such a road from Hollywood to Glendalough.

Bullaun Stones

Bullaun is the Irish word for a stone with one, though sometimes multiple, man-made concave depressions in its upper surface, which is usually raised somewhat above ground level. Such stones are frequently found on old Irish monastic sites, and a considerable number are known from the area in and around Glendalough. Various explanations have been offered for their original function – baptismal fonts, or mortars for grinding barley, crushing vegetables or even ore. But the cavities often gather water which was considered to help in removing warts, and legend suggests that the Deer Stone at Glendalough was used to hold milk for St. Kevin. The considerable number of such stones at Glendalough, and their presence at other notable pilgrimage sites such as Clonmacnois, would lend support to the idea that bullaun stones were used to accumulate water with which the pilgrims could have blessed themselves in the hope of a cure for some bodily ailment, and the frequently-used name 'wart stone' is the modern survival of some such old tradition.

Turlough Hill Electricity Generating Station

The skyline on any walk up to the Wicklow Gap is dominated by an unexpectedly flat top to one of the surrounding hills, and this is due to the rim of a hill-top reservoir forming part of a pumped storage scheme operated by the Electricity Supply Board. The reservoir on Turlough Hill has a capacity of 2.3 million cubic meters, its water covering an area of 20 acres. Almost one million cubic meters of peat, as well as 2.5 million tons of rock, had to be removed before it could be built. This water flows down inside the mountain through a pressure shaft, and then into a turbine before finally draining out into a glacial lake, Lough Nahanagan, which can be seen from the Wicklow Gap. The electricity is generated in this way at peak times, and some of it is then used to pump the water back up to the reservoir when demand is slack: a very cost-efficient method of providing power for domestic and industrial use when it is most needed. Built between 1970 and 1974, Turlough Hill was the largest civil engineering operation ever undertaken in Ireland.

Imogen Stuart's *St. Kevin* near the Upper lake at Glendalough

THE LEAD MINES

Mining for copper, lead and zinc had begun in the Glendalough area by the early nineteenth century if not before and, by 1837, the annual output had reached 11,000 tons of lead ore. Today, visible remains of the workings can be seen at two locations, one on the north-western slopes of Camaderry mountain and the other at the top of the Glendalough valley, both said to have been linked by shafts going underneath the mountain. The first virtually straddles St. Kevin's Road more than a mile downhill from Lough Nahanagan and still preserves remains of a mill-race for an ore-grinding mill, as well as a smelting operation. The surviving spoil-heaps contain crystals of various minerals including barites, chalcopyrite, malachite, azurite and, of course, galena or lead, which was the mines' main product. One of the surviving granite buildings housed a water wheel which drove rollers and iron-shod pestles to crush the ore before it was separated from the waste material or gangue, work partially carried out by women and children on what were known as 'picking floors'. The members of the mining community, said to have numbered 800 at one stage, were renowned for their singing and violin playing.

ACKNOWLEDGEMENTS:

The Heritage Council would like to thank a number of bodies and individuals who have worked so hard to make Slí Chaoimhín - St. Kevin's Way such a successful reality, and whose assistance has been invaluable in the production of this booklet. Prime among these is the Slí Chaoimhín - St. Kevin's Way Committee, under the enthuastic chairmanship of Willie Mullen, and comprising the following members: Rev. Michael Begg, Anne Clancy, Denis Connolly, Peter Corrigan, Aidan Cruise, Peter Graham, Jim Kennedy, Dr. Jim Lydon, Frances McDermott, Tomás Maher, Brid Mahon, Sr. Genevieve Mooney, O.P., Sean Nugent, Steve Ryan, Terry Spillane and Eleanor Sutherland.
Coillte, under its Forestry Manager, Jim Fanning, and ably assisted by Tom Donahoe, Willie Doyle, Jim Halpin, Sean Hayes, Pat Kelly, Noel Murphy, Michael O'Brien, Frank Reid and Seamus Ward have gone beyond the normal call of duty in smoothening the walkers' ground by installing paths and bridges on their extensive landholdings over which the route passes.
The assistance of Dúchas staff members Wesley Atkins, Monica Byrne, Sean Casey, Con Manning, Enda Mullen and Edward Ward is also much appreciated in ensuring that proper standards are maintained, and Seamus Doyle, Declan Geraghty, Jack Keogh, Michael Mangan and Tony O'Neill of the Wicklow County Council have been of great help in facilitating the creation of St. Kevin's Way.
The whole project would not have been possible without the willing co-operation of the following landowners who have kindly agreed to allow the walkers go over their property: Mark and Kit Byrne, Peter and Alice Byrne, Andy Corrigan, Harry Farrington, Paul Murphy and Liam Robinson. Their public spiritedness deserves a clap from every participant in the walk. Generous advice was given by Andy Halpin and Myles Clarke, and the whole project was blessed by Rev. Fr. Prendergast, P.P. of Hollywood, Rev. Eric Greaves, Church of Ireland, Hollywood, and Fr. O'Toole, P.P. of Glendalough.

Bibliography

Anon. 'Ancient Pilgrim Road excavated at Turlough Hill', *Electrical Mail*, August 1972, p.1.

Anon. 'Some notes on the investigations at St. Kevin's Road', *Electrical Mail*, September 1972, page 6.

Anon. *Exploring Glendalough*. Heritage Service (no date).

Anon. *Glendalough, Visitors' Guide*. Dúchas, the Heritage Service (no date).

Anon. *Turlough Hill pumped storage scheme*. Electricity Supply Board (no date).

Barrow, Lennox. *Glendalough and St. Kevin*, Dundalk 1972.

Crawford, W.H. 'The patron, or festival of St. Kevin at the Seven Churches, Glendalough, County Wicklow 1813', *Ulster Folklife* 32, 1986, pp. 37-47.

Dick, William. 'Dressing ore at Wicklow Gap', *Technology Ireland* April 1972.

Harbison, Peter. *Pilgrimage in Ireland. The Monuments and the People*. London 1991.

Leask, Harold G. *Glendalough, Co. Wicklow. Official historical & descriptive guide*. Stationery Office, Dublin (no date).

Lucas, A.T. 'Toghers or causeways: some evidence from archaeological, literary, historical and place-name sources', *Proceedings of the Royal Irish Academy* 85 C, 1985, pp. 37-60.

Orpen, Goddard H. 'The Holywood stone and the labyrinth of Knossos', *Journal of the Royal Society of Antiquaries of Ireland* 53, 1923, pp. 177-89.

Price, Liam. 'Glendalough: St. Kevin's Road', in (ed.) E. Ua Riain (John Ryan), *Féil-Sgríbhinn Eóin Mhic Néill*, Dublin 1940, pp. 244-71.

Price, Liam. 'Rock-basins or, 'bullauns', at Glendalough and elsewhere', *Journal of the Royal Society of Antiquaries of Ireland* 89, 1959, pp. 161-88.

Price, Liam, The Place-names of County Wicklow, Vols. 1 and 4, Dublin 1945 and 1953 respectively.

Rodgers, Michael and Marcus Losack. *Glendalough, A Celtic Pilgrimage*, Dublin 1996.